I0492362

The Constitution of
The State of Utah:
A Quick Reference Guide

Bootblack Budget Books
Copyright 2018 ©
ISBN-13: 978-1724416704
ISBN-10: 1724416707

Contents:

Article II: State Boundaries – Page 36

Section 1: State Boundaries

Article III: Ordinance – Page 37

First: Religious Toleration - Polygamy Forbidden

Second: Right to Public Domain Disclaimed - Taxation of Lands - Exemption

Third: Territorial Debts Assumed

Forth: Free, Nonsectarian schools

Article V: Distribution of Powers – Page 42

Section 1: Three Departments of Government

Article VIII: Judicial Department – Page 69

Article IX: Congressional and Legislative Apportionment – Page 75

Section 1: Dividing the state into Districts

Section 2: Number of Members of Legislature

Article X: Education – Page 76

Article XIII: Revenue and Taxation – Page 88

Article XIV: Public Debt – Page 97

Section 1: Fixing the Limit of the State Indebtedness/Exceptions

Section 2: Debts for Public Defense

Section 3: Certain Debt of Counties, Cities, Towns, School Districts, and other Political Subdivisions not to Exceed Taxes/Exception/Debt may be Incurred only for Specified Purposes

Section 4: Limit of Indebtedness of Counties, Cities, Towns, and School Districts/Larger Indebtedness may be Allowed

Section 5: Borrowed Money to be Applied to Authorized Use

Section 6: State not to Assume County, City, Town or School District Debts /Exception

Section 7: Existing Indebtedness not Impaired

Article XV: Militia – Page 100

Section 1: How Constituted

Section 2: Organization and Equipment

Article XVI: Labor – Page 101

Article XVII: Water Rights – Page 103

Section 1. Existing Rights Confirmed

Article XVIII: Forestry – Page 104

Section 1: Forests to be Preserved

Article XX: Public Lands – Page 105

Section 1: Land Grants Accepted on Terms of Trust

Section 2: School and Institutional Trust Lands

Article XXII: Miscellaneous – Page 106

Section 1: Homestead Exemption

Section 3: Seat of Government

Section 4: State Trust Fund/Principal to be Held in Perpetuity/Use of Income

Section 5: Officers may not Profit

Article XXIV: Schedule – Page 110

Preamble

Grateful to Almighty God for life and liberty, we, the people of Utah, in order to secure and perpetuate the principles of free government, do ordain and establish this CONSTITUTION.

ARTICLE I: DECLARATION OF RIGHTS

Section 1. Inherent and Inalienable Rights

All men have the inherent and inalienable right to enjoy and defend their lives and liberties; to acquire, possess and protect property; to worship according to the dictates of their consciences; to assemble peaceably, protest against wrongs, and petition for redress of grievances; to communicate freely their thoughts and opinions, being responsible for the abuse of that right.

Section 2. All Political Power Inherent in the People

All political power is inherent in the people; and all free governments are founded on their authority for their equal protection and benefit, and they have the right to alter or reform their government as the public welfare may require.

Section 3. Utah Inseparable from the Union

The State of Utah is an inseparable part of the Federal Union and the Constitution of the United States is the supreme law of the land.

Section 4. Religious Liberty

The rights of conscience shall never be infringed. The State shall make no law respecting an establishment of religion or prohibiting the free exercise thereof; no religious test shall be required as a qualification for any office of public trust or for any vote at any election; nor shall any person be incompetent as a witness or juror on account of religious belief or the absence thereof. There shall be no union of Church and State, nor shall any church dominate the State or interfere with its functions. No public money or property shall be appropriated for or applied to any religious worship, exercise or instruction, or for the support of any ecclesiastical establishment.

Section 5. Habeas Corpus

The privilege of the writ of habeas corpus shall not be suspended, unless, in case of rebellion or invasion, the public safety requires it.

Section 6. Right to Bear Arms

The individual right of the people to keep and bear arms for security and defense of self, family, others, property, or the state, as well as for other lawful purposes shall not be infringed; but nothing herein shall prevent the Legislature from defining the lawful use of arms.

Section 7. Due Process of Law

No person shall be deprived of life, liberty or property, without due process of law.

Section 8. Offenses Bailable

(1) All persons charged with a crime shall be bailable except:

(a) persons charged with a capital offense when there is substantial evidence to support the charge; or

(b) persons charged with a felony while on probation or parole, or while free on bail awaiting trial on a previous felony charge, when there is substantial evidence to support the new felony charge; or

(c) persons charged with any other crime, designated by statute as one for which bail may be denied, if there is substantial evidence to support the charge and the court finds by clear and convincing evidence that the person would constitute a substantial danger to any other person or to the community or is likely to flee the jurisdiction of the court if released on bail.

(2) Persons convicted of a crime are bailable pending appeal only as prescribed by law.

Section 9. Excessive Bail and Fines/Cruel Punishments

Excessive bail shall not be required; excessive fines shall not be imposed; nor shall cruel and unusual punishments be inflicted. Persons arrested or imprisoned shall not be treated with unnecessary rigor.

Section 10. Trial by Jury

In capital cases the right of trial by jury shall remain inviolate. In capital cases the jury shall consist of twelve persons, and in all other felony cases, the jury shall consist of no fewer than eight persons. In other cases, the Legislature shall establish the number of jurors by statute, but in no event shall a jury consist of fewer than four persons. In criminal cases the verdict shall be unanimous. In civil cases three-fourths of the jurors may find a verdict. A jury in civil cases shall be waived unless demanded.

Section 11. Courts Open/Redress of Injuries

All courts shall be open, and every person, for an injury done to him in his person, property or reputation, shall have remedy by due course of law, which shall be administered without denial or unnecessary delay; and no person shall be barred from prosecuting or defending before any tribunal in this State, by himself or counsel, any civil cause to which he is a party.

Section 12. Rights of Accused Persons

In criminal prosecutions the accused shall have the right to appear and defend in person and by counsel, to demand the nature and cause of the accusation against him, to have a copy thereof, to testify in his own behalf, to be confronted by the witnesses against him, to have compulsory process to compel the attendance of witnesses in his own behalf, to have a speedy public trial by an impartial jury of the county or district in which the offense is alleged to have been committed, and the right to appeal in all cases. In no instance shall any accused person, before final judgment, be compelled to advance money or fees to secure the rights herein guaranteed. The accused shall not be compelled to give evidence against himself; a wife shall not be compelled to testify against her husband, nor a husband against his wife, nor shall any person be twice put in jeopardy for the same offense.

Where the defendant is otherwise entitled to a preliminary examination, the function of that examination is limited to determining whether probable cause exists unless otherwise provided by statute. Nothing in this constitution shall preclude the use of reliable hearsay evidence as defined by statute or rule in whole or in part at any preliminary examination to determine probable cause or at any pretrial proceeding with respect to release of the defendant if appropriate discovery is allowed as defined by statute or rule.

Section 13. Prosecution by Information or Indictment/Grand Jury

Offenses heretofore required to be prosecuted by indictment, shall be prosecuted by information after examination and commitment by a magistrate, unless the examination be waived by the accused with the consent of the State, or by indictment, with or without such examination and commitment. The formation of the grand jury and the powers and duties thereof shall be as prescribed by the Legislature.

Section 14. Unreasonable Searches Forbidden/Issuance of Warrant

The right of the people to be secure in their persons, houses, papers and effects against unreasonable searches and seizures shall not be violated; and no warrant shall issue but upon probable cause supported by oath or affirmation, particularly describing the place to be searched, and the person or thing to be seized.

Section 15. Freedom of Speech and of the Press/Libel

No law shall be passed to abridge or restrain the freedom of speech or of the press. In all criminal prosecutions for libel the truth may be given in evidence to the jury; and if it shall appear to the jury that the matter charged as libelous is true, and was published with good motives, and for justifiable ends, the party shall be acquitted; and the jury shall have the right to determine the law and the fact.

Section 16. No Imprisonment for Debt/Exception

There shall be no imprisonment for debt except in cases of absconding debtors.

Section 17. Elections to be Free/Soldiers Voting

All elections shall be free, and no power, civil or military, shall at any time interfere to prevent the free exercise of the right of suffrage. Soldiers, in time of war, may vote at their post of duty, in or out of the State, under regulations to be prescribed by law.

Section 18. Attainder/Ex Post Facto Laws/Impairing Contracts

No bill of attainder, ex post facto law, or law impairing the obligation of contracts shall be passed.

Section 19. Treason Defined/Proof

Treason against the State shall consist only in levying war against it, or in adhering to its enemies or in giving them aid and comfort. No person shall be convicted of treason unless on the testimony of two witnesses to the same overt act.

Section 20. Military Subordinate to the Civil Power

The military shall be in strict subordination to the civil power, and no soldier in time of peace, shall be quartered in any house without the consent of the owner; nor in time of war except in a manner to be prescribed by law.

Section 21. Slavery Forbidden

Neither slavery nor involuntary servitude, except as a punishment for crime, whereof the party shall have been duly convicted, shall exist within this State.

Section 22. Private Property for Public Use

Private property shall not be taken or damaged for public use without just compensation.

Section 23. Irrevocable Franchises Forbidden

No law shall be passed granting irrevocably any franchise, privilege or immunity.

Section 24. Uniform Operation of Laws

All laws of a general nature shall have uniform operation.

Section 25. Rights Retained by People

This enumeration of rights shall not be construed to impair or deny others retained by the people.

Section 26. Provisions Mandatory and Prohibitory

The provisions of this Constitution are mandatory and prohibitory, unless by express words they are declared to be otherwise.

Section 27. Fundamental Rights

Frequent recurrence to fundamental principles is essential to the security of individual rights and the perpetuity of free government.

Section 28. Declaration of the Rights of Crime Victims

(1) To preserve and protect victims' rights to justice and due process, victims of crimes have these rights, as defined by law:

(a) To be treated with fairness, respect, and dignity, and to be free from harassment and abuse throughout the criminal justice process;

(b) Upon request, to be informed of, be present at, and to be heard at important criminal justice hearings related to the victim, either in person or through a lawful representative, once a criminal information or indictment charging a crime has been publicly filed in court; and

(c) To have a sentencing judge, for the purpose of imposing an appropriate sentence, receive and consider, without evidentiary limitation, reliable information concerning the background, character, and conduct of a person convicted of an offense except that this subsection does not apply to capital cases or situations involving privileges.

(2) Nothing in this section shall be construed as creating a cause of action for money damages, costs, or attorney's fees, or for dismissing any criminal charge, or relief from any criminal judgment.

(3) The provisions of this section shall extend to all felony crimes and such other crimes or acts, including juvenile offenses, as the Legislature may provide.

(4) The Legislature shall have the power to enforce and define this section by statute.

Section 29. Marriage

Marriage consists only of the legal union between a man and a woman.

No other domestic union, however denominated, may be recognized as a marriage or given the same or substantially equivalent legal effect.

Article II: State Boundaries

Section 1. State Boundaries

The boundaries of the State of Utah shall be as follows:
Beginning at a point formed by the intersection of the thirty-second degree of longitude west from Washington, with the thirty-seventh degree of north latitude; thence due west along said thirty-seventh degree of north latitude to the intersection of the same with the thirty-seventh degree of longitude west from Washington; thence due north along said thirty-seventh degree of west longitude to the intersection of the same with the forty-second degree of north latitude; thence due east along said forty-second degree of north latitude to the intersection of the same with the thirty-fourth degree of longitude west from Washington; thence due south along said thirty-fourth degree of west longitude to the intersection of the same with the forty-first degree of north latitude; thence due east along said forty-first degree of north latitude to the intersection of the same with the thirty-second degree of longitude west from Washington; thence due south along said thirty-second degree of west longitude to the place of beginning.

Article III: Ordinance

The following ordinance shall be irrevocable without the consent of the United States and the people of this State:

First: Religious Toleration/Polygamy Forbidden

Perfect toleration of religious sentiment is guaranteed. No inhabitant of this State shall ever be molested in person or property on account of his or her mode of religious worship; but polygamous or plural marriages are forever prohibited.

Second: Right to Public Domain Disclaimed/Taxation of Lands/Exemption

The people inhabiting this State do affirm and declare that they forever disclaim all right and title to the unappropriated public lands lying within the boundaries hereof, and to all lands lying within said limits owned or held by any Indian or Indian tribes, and that until the title thereto shall have been extinguished by the United States, the same shall be and remain subject to the disposition of the United States, and said Indian lands shall remain under the absolute jurisdiction and control of the Congress of the United States. The lands belonging to citizens of the United States, residing without this State shall never be taxed at a higher rate than the lands belonging to residents of this State; but nothing in this ordinance shall preclude this state from taxing, as other lands are taxed, any lands owned or held by any Indian who has severed his tribal relations, and has obtained from the United States or from any person, by patent or other grant, a title thereto, save and except such lands as have been or may be granted to any Indian or Indians under any act of Congress, containing a provision exempting the lands thus granted from taxation, which last mentioned lands shall be exempt from taxation so long, and to such extent, as is or may be provided in the act of Congress granting the same.

Third: Territorial Debts Assumed

All debts and liabilities of the Territory of Utah, incurred by authority of the Legislative Assembly thereof, are hereby assumed and shall be paid by this State.

Fourth: Free, Nonsectarian schools

The Legislature shall make laws for the establishment and maintenance of a system of public schools, which shall be open to all the children of the State and be free from sectarian control.

ARTICLE IV: ELECTIONS AND RIGHT OF SUFFRAGE

Section 1. Equal Political Rights

The rights of citizens of the State of Utah to vote and hold office shall not be denied or abridged on account of sex. Both male and female citizens of this State shall enjoy equally all civil, political and religious rights and privileges.

Section 2. Qualifications to Vote

Every citizen of the United States, eighteen years of age or over, who makes proper proof of residence in this state for thirty days next preceding any election, or for such other period as required by law, shall be entitled to vote in the election.

Section 3. Voters/Immunity from Arrest

In all cases except those of treason, felony or breach of the peace, voters shall be privileged from arrest on the days of election, during their attendance at elections, and going to and returning therefrom.

Section 4. Voters/Immunity from Militia Duty

No voter shall be obliged to perform militia duty on the day of election except in time of war or public danger.

Section 5. Voters to be Citizens of United States

No person shall be deemed a qualified voter of this State unless such person be a citizen of the United States.

Section 6. Mentally Incompetent Persons, Convicted Felons, and Certain Criminals Ineligible to Vote

Any mentally incompetent person, any person convicted of a felony, or any person convicted of treason or a crime against the elective franchise, may not be permitted to vote at any election or be eligible to hold office in this State until the right to vote or hold elective office is restored as provided by statute.

Section 7. Property Qualification Forbidden

No property qualification shall be required for any person to vote or hold office.

Section 8. Election to be by Secret Ballot

(1) All elections, including elections under state or federal law for public office, on an initiative or referendum, or to designate or authorize employee representation or individual representation, shall be by secret ballot.

(2) Nothing in this section may be construed to prevent the use of any machine or mechanical contrivance for the purpose of receiving and registering the votes cast at any election, as long as secrecy in voting is preserved.

Section 9. General and Special Elections/Terms/Election of Local Officers

(1) Each general election shall be held on the Tuesday next following the first Monday in November of each even-numbered year.

(2) Special elections may be held as provided by statute.

(3) The term of each officer, except legislator, elected at a general election shall commence on the first Monday in January next following the date of the election.

(4) The election of officers of each city, town, school district, and other political subdivision of the State shall be held at the time and in the manner provided by statute.

Section 10. Oath of Office

All officers made elective or appointive by this Constitution or by the laws made in pursuance thereof, before entering upon the duties of their respective offices, shall take and subscribe the following oath or affirmation: "I do solemnly swear (or affirm) that I will support, obey, and defend the Constitution of the United States and the Constitution of the State of Utah, and that I will discharge the duties of my office with fidelity.

ARTICLE V: DISTRIBUTION OF POWERS

Section 1. Three Departments of Government

The powers of the government of the State of Utah shall be divided into three distinct departments, the Legislative, the Executive, and the Judicial; and no person charged with the exercise of powers properly belonging to one of these departments, shall exercise any functions appertaining to either of the others, except in the cases herein expressly directed or permitted.

ARTICLE VI: LEGISLATIVE DEPARTMENT

Section 1. Power Vested in Senate, House, and People

(1) The Legislative power of the State shall be vested in:

(a) a Senate and House of Representatives which shall be designated the Legislature of the State of Utah; and

(b) the people of the State of Utah as provided in Subsection (2).

(2) (a) (i) The legal voters of the State of Utah, in the numbers, under the conditions, in the manner, and within the time provided by statute, may:

(A) initiate any desired legislation and cause it to be submitted to the people for adoption upon a majority vote of those voting on the legislation, as provided by statute; or

(B) require any law passed by the Legislature, except those laws passed by a two-thirds vote of the members elected to each house of the Legislature, to be submitted to the voters of the State, as provided by statute, before the law may take effect.

(ii) Notwithstanding Subsection (2)(a)(i)(A), legislation initiated to allow, limit, or prohibit the taking of wildlife or the season for or method of taking wildlife shall be adopted upon approval of two-thirds of those voting.

(b) The legal voters of any county, city, or town, in the numbers, under the conditions, in the manner, and within the time provided by statute, may:

(i) initiate any desired legislation and cause it to be submitted to the people of the county, city, or town for adoption upon a majority vote of those voting on the legislation, as provided by statute; or

(ii) require any law or ordinance passed by the law making body of the county, city, or town to be submitted to the voters thereof, as provided by statute, before the law or ordinance may take effect.

Section 2. Time of General Sessions

Annual general sessions of the Legislature shall be held at the seat of government and shall begin on the fourth Monday in January.

Section 3. Election of House Members/Terms

(1) The members of the House of Representatives shall be chosen biennially on even-numbered years by the qualified voters of the respective representative districts, on the first Tuesday after the first Monday in November.

(2) Their term of office shall be two years from the first day of January next after their election.

Section 4. Election of Senators/Terms

(1) The senators shall be chosen by the qualified voters of the respective senatorial districts, at the same times and places as members of the House of Representatives.

(2) Their term of office shall be four years from the first day of January next after their election.

(3) As nearly one-half as may be practicable shall be elected in each biennium as the Legislature shall determine by law with each apportionment.

Section 5. Who is Eligible as a Legislator

(1) A person is not eligible to the office of senator or representative unless the person is:

(a) a citizen of the United States;

(b) at least twenty-five years of age;

(c) a qualified voter in the district from which the person is chosen;

(d) a resident of the state for three consecutive years immediately prior to:

(i) the last date provided by statute for filing for the office, for a person seeking election to the office; or

(ii) the person's appointment to the office, for a person appointed to fill a mid-term vacancy; and

(e) (i) a resident of the district from which the person is elected for six consecutive months immediately prior to the last date provided by statute for filing for the office; or

(ii) a resident of the district for which the person is appointed to fill a mid-term vacancy for six consecutive months immediately prior to the person's appointment.

(2) A person elected or appointed to the office of senator or representative may not continue to serve in that office after ceasing to be a resident of the district from which elected or for which appointed.

Section 6. Who Ineligible as Legislator

No person holding any public office of profit or trust under authority of the United States, or of this State, shall be a member of the Legislature: Provided That appointments in the State Militia, and the offices of notary public, justice of the peace, United States commissioner, and postmaster of the fourth class, shall not, within the meaning of this section, be considered offices of profit or trust.

Section 7. Ineligibility of Legislator to Office Created at Term for Which Elected

No member of the Legislature, during the term for which he was elected, shall be appointed or elected to any civil office of profit under this State, which shall have been created, or the emoluments of which shall have been increased, during the term for which he was elected.

Section 8. Legislator, Privilege from Arrest

Members of the Legislature, in all cases except treason, felony or breach of the peace, shall be privileged from arrest during each session of the Legislature, for fifteen days next preceding each session, and in returning therefrom; and for words used in any speech or debate in either house, they shall not be questioned in any other place.

Section 9. Compensation of Legislators/Citizens Salary Commission

The Legislature shall not increase the salaries of its members on its own initiative, but shall provide by law for the appointment by the Governor of a citizens' salary commission to make recommendations concerning the salaries of members of the Legislature. Upon submission of the commission's recommendations, the Legislature shall by law accept, reject or lower the salary but may not, in any event, increase the recommendation. The Legislature shall provide by law for the expenses of its members. Until salaries and expenses enacted as authorized by this section become effective, members of the Legislature shall receive compensation of $25 per diem while actually in session, expenses of $15 per diem while actually in session, and mileage as provided by law.

Section 10. Each House to be Judge of Election and Qualifications of its Members/Expulsion/Legislative Ethics Commission

(1) Each house shall be the judge of the election and qualifications of its members, and may punish them for disorderly conduct, and with the concurrence of two-thirds of all the members elected, expel a member for cause.

(2) (a) There is established a legislative ethics commission with authority to conduct an independent review of each complaint alleging unethical legislative behavior, to determine whether the complaint merits further consideration by the house of the member against whom the complaint is made.

(b) (i) The commission shall consist of five members.

(ii) A commission member may not be a sitting legislator or a person who is registered as a lobbyist.

(c) The Legislature may by rule provide for:

(i) procedures and requirements for filing a complaint alleging unethical legislative behavior;

(ii) the qualifications, appointment, and terms of commission members; and

(iii) commission duties, powers, operations, and procedures.

Section 11. Majority is Quorum/Attendance Compelled

A majority of the members of each house shall constitute a quorum to transact business, but a smaller number may adjourn from day to day, and may compel the attendance of absent members in such manner and under such penalties as each house may prescribe.

Section 12. Rules/Choosing Officers and Employees

Each house shall determine the rules of its proceedings and choose its own officers and employees.

Section 13. Vacancies to be Filled

Vacancies that may occur in either house of the legislature shall be filled in such manner as may be provided by law.

Section 14. Journals/Yeas and Nays

Each house shall keep a journal of its proceedings, which, except in case of executive sessions, shall be published, and the yeas and nays on any question, at the request of five members of such house, shall be entered upon the journal.

Section 15. Sessions to be public/Adjournments

All sessions of the Legislature, except those of the Senate while sitting in executive session, shall be public; and neither house, without the consent of the other, shall adjourn for more than three days, nor to any other place than that in which it may be holding session.

Section 16. Duration of Sessions

(1) Except in cases of impeachment, no annual general session of the Legislature may exceed 45 calendar days, excluding federal holidays.

(2) No session of the Legislature convened by the Governor under Article VII, Section 6 may exceed 30 calendar days, except in cases of impeachment.

Section 17. Impeachment by House

(1) The House of Representatives shall have the sole power of impeachment, but in order to impeach, two-thirds of all the members elected must vote therefore.

(2) If not already convened in an annual general session, the House of Representatives may convene for the purpose of impeachment if a poll of members conducted by the Speaker of the House indicates that two-thirds of the members of the House of Representatives are in favor of convening.

Section 18. Trial of Impeachment by Senate

(1) All impeachments shall be tried by the Senate, and senators, when sitting for that purpose, shall take oath or make affirmation to do justice according to the law and the evidence.

(2) Upon an impeachment by the House of Representatives, the Senate shall, if not already convened in an annual general session, convene for the purpose of trying the impeachment.

(3) When the Governor is on trial, the Chief Justice of the Supreme Court shall preside.

(4) No person shall be convicted without the concurrence of two-thirds of the senators elected.

Section 19. Officers Liable for Impeachment / Judgment / Prosecution by Law

The Governor and other State and Judicial officers shall be liable to impeachment for high crimes, misdemeanors, or malfeasance in office; but judgment in such cases shall extend only to removal from office and disqualification to hold any office of honor, trust, or profit in the State. The party, whether convicted or acquitted, shall, nevertheless, be liable to prosecution, trial, and punishment according to law.

Section 20. Service of Articles of Impeachment

No person shall be tried on impeachment, unless he shall have been served with a copy of the articles thereof, at least ten days before the trial, and after such service he shall not exercise the duties of his office until he shall have been acquitted.

Section 21. Removal of Officers

All officers not liable to impeachment shall be removed for any of the offenses specified in this article, in such manner as may be provided by law.

Section 22. Reading of Bills/Bill to Contain only one Subject/Bills Passed by Majority

Every bill shall be read by title three separate times in each house except in cases where two-thirds of the house where such bill is pending suspend this requirement. Except general appropriation bills and bills for the codification and general revision of laws, no bill shall be passed containing more than one subject, which shall be clearly expressed in its title. The vote upon the final passage of all bills shall be by yeas and nays and entered upon the respective journals of the house in which the vote occurs. No bill or joint resolution shall be passed except with the assent of the majority of all the members elected to each house of the Legislature.

Section 24. Presiding Officers to Sign Bills

The presiding officer of each house, not later than five days following adjournment, shall sign all bills and joint resolutions passed by the Legislature, certifying to their accuracy and authenticity as enacted by the Legislature.

Section 25. Publication of Acts/Effective Dates of Acts

All acts shall be officially published, and no act shall take effect until sixty days after the adjournment of the session at which it passed, unless the Legislature by a vote of two-thirds of all the members elected to each house, shall otherwise direct.

Section 26. Private Laws Forbidden

No private or special law shall be enacted where a general law can be applicable.

Section 27. Games of Chance not Authorized

The Legislature shall not authorize any game of chance, lottery or gift enterprise under any pretense or for any purpose.

Section 28. Special Privileges Forbidden

The Legislature shall not delegate to any special commission, private corporation or association, any power to make, supervise or interfere with any municipal improvement, money, property or effects, whether held in trust or otherwise, to levy taxes, to select a capitol site, or to perform any municipal functions.

Section 29. Lending Public Credit and Subscribing to Stock or Bonds Forbidden/Exception

(1) Neither the State nor any county, city, town, school district, or other political subdivision of the State may lend its credit or, except as provided in Subsection (2), subscribe to stock or bonds in aid of any private individual or corporate enterprise or undertaking.

(2) Except as otherwise provided by statute, the State or a public institution of post-secondary education may acquire an equity interest in a private business entity as consideration for the sale, license, or other transfer to the private business entity of intellectual property developed in whole or in part by the State or the public institution of post-secondary education, and may hold or dispose of the equity interest.

Section 30. Continuity in Government

(1) Notwithstanding any general or special provisions of the Constitution, in order to insure continuity of state and local government operations when such operations are seriously disrupted as a result of natural or man-made disaster or disaster caused by enemy attack, the Legislature may:

(a) provide for prompt and temporary succession to the powers and duties of any elected or appointed public office, the incumbents of which may become unavailable for carrying on the powers and duties of such offices; and

(b) adopt measures necessary and proper for insuring the continuity of governmental operations including, but not limited to, the financing thereof.

(2) Subsection (1) does not permit these temporary public officers to act or these temporary measures to be contrary to the Constitution and applicable law.

Section 31. Additional Compensation of Legislators

For attendance at meetings of interim committees established by law to function between legislative sessions, members of the Legislature shall receive additional per diem compensation and mileage at a rate not to exceed that provided in this Constitution for regular legislative sessions.

Section 32. Appointment of Additional Employees/Legal Counsel

(1) The Legislature may appoint temporary or permanent nonmember employees for work during and between sessions.

(2) The Legislature may appoint legal counsel which shall provide and control all legal services for the Legislature unless otherwise provided by statute.

Section 33. Legislative Auditor Appointed

The Legislature shall appoint a legislative auditor to serve at its pleasure. The legislative auditor shall have authority to conduct audits of any funds, functions, and accounts in any branch, department, agency or political subdivision of this state and shall perform such other related duties as may be prescribed by the Legislature. He shall report to and be answerable only to the Legislature.

Article VII: Executive Department

Section 1. Executive Department Officers/Terms, Residence, and Duties

(1) The elective constitutional officers of the Executive Department shall consist of Governor, Lieutenant Governor, State Auditor, State Treasurer, and Attorney General.

(2) Each officer shall:

(a) hold office for four years beginning on the first Monday of January next after their election;

(b) during their terms of office reside within the state; and

(c) perform such duties as are prescribed by this Constitution and as provided by statute.

Section 2. Election of Officers/Governor and Lieutenant Governor Elected Jointly

(1) The officers provided for in Section 1 shall be elected by the qualified voters of the state at the time and place of voting for members of the Legislature. The candidates respectively having the highest number of votes cast for the office voted for shall be elected. If two or more candidates have an equal and the highest number of votes for any one of the offices, the two houses of the Legislature at its next session shall elect by joint ballot one of those candidates for that office.

(2) In the election the names of the candidates for Governor and Lieutenant Governor for each political party shall appear together on the ballot and the votes cast for a candidate for Governor shall be considered as also cast for the candidate for Lieutenant Governor.

Section 3. Qualifications of Officers

(1) To be eligible for the office of Governor or Lieutenant Governor a person shall be 30 years of age or older at the time of election.

(2) To be eligible for the office of Attorney General a person shall be 25 years of age or older, at the time of election, admitted to practice before the Supreme Court of the State of Utah, and in good standing at the bar.

(3) To be eligible for the office of State Auditor or State Treasurer a person shall be 25 years of age or older at the time of election.

(4) No person is eligible to any of the offices provided for in Section 1 unless at the time of election that person is a qualified voter and has been a resident citizen of the state for five years next preceding the election.

Section 4. Governor Commander-in-chief

The Governor shall be Commander-in-Chief of the military forces of the State, except when they shall be called into the service of the United States. The Governor shall have power to call out the militia to execute the laws, to suppress insurrection, or to repel invasion.

Section 5. Executive Power Vested in Governor/Duties/Legal Counsel

(1) The executive power of the state shall be vested in the Governor who shall see that the laws are faithfully executed.

(2) The Governor shall transact all executive business with the officers of the government, civil and military, and may require information in writing from the officers of the Executive Department, and from the officers and managers of state institutions upon any subject relating to the condition, management, and expenses of their respective offices and institutions. The Governor may at any time when the Legislature is not in session, if deemed necessary, appoint a committee to investigate and report to the Governor upon the condition of any executive office or state institution.

(3) The Governor shall communicate by message the condition of the state to the Legislature at every annual general session and recommend such measures as may be deemed expedient.

(4) The Governor may appoint legal counsel to advise the Governor.

Section 6. Convening of extra sessions of Legislature/Advance public notice.

(1) (a) On extraordinary occasions, the Governor may convene the Legislature by proclamation, in which shall be stated the purpose for which the Legislature is to be convened, and it may transact no legislative business except that for which it was especially convened, or such other legislative business as the Governor may call to its attention while in session, subject to Subsection (1)(b). The Legislature, however, may provide for the expenses of the session and other matters incidental thereto.

(b) The Legislature may not transact any legislative business in a special session convened under Subsection (1)(a) for which the Governor has not provided 48 hours advance public notice, except in cases of declared emergency or with the concurrence of two-thirds of all members elected to each house.

(2) The Governor may also by proclamation convene the Senate in extraordinary session for the transaction of executive business.

Section 7. Adjournment of Legislature by Governor

In case of a disagreement between the two houses of the Legislature at any special session, with respect to the time of adjournment, the Governor shall have power to adjourn the Legislature to such time as the Governor may think proper if it is not beyond the time fixed for the convening of the next Legislature.

Section 8. Bills Presented to Governor for Approval and Veto/Items of Appropriation/Legislative Session to Consider Vetoed Items

(1) Each bill passed by the Legislature, before it becomes a law, shall be presented to the governor. If the bill is approved, the governor shall sign it, and thereupon it shall become a law. If the bill is disapproved, it shall be returned with the governor's objections to the house in which it originated. That house shall then enter the objections upon its journal and proceed to reconsider the bill. If upon reconsideration the bill again passes both houses by a yea and nay vote of two-thirds of the members elected to each house, it shall become a law.

(2) If any bill is not returned by the governor within ten days after it has been presented to the governor, Sunday and the day it was received excepted, it shall become a law without a signature. If legislative adjournment prevents return of the bill, it shall become a law unless the governor within twenty days after adjournment files the objections to it with such officers as provided by law.

(3) The governor may disapprove any item of appropriation contained in any bill while approving other portions of the bill. In such case the governor shall append to the bill at the time of signing it a statement of the item or items which are disapproved, together with the reasons for disapproval, and the item or items may not take effect unless passed over the governor's objections as provided in this section.

(4) If the governor disapproves any bill or item of appropriation after the adjournment sine die of any session of the Legislature, the presiding officer of each house shall poll the members of that house on the matter of reconvening the Legislature. If two-thirds of the members of each house are in favor of reconvening, the Legislature shall be convened in a session that shall begin within 60 days after the adjournment of the session at which the disapproved bill or item of appropriation passed. This session may not exceed five calendar days and shall be convened at a time set jointly by the presiding officer of each house solely for the purpose of reconsidering the bill or item of appropriation disapproved. If upon reconsideration, the bill or item of appropriation again passes both houses of the Legislature by a yea and nay vote of two-thirds of the members elected to each house, the bill shall become law or the item of appropriation shall take effect on the original effective date of the law or item of appropriation.

Section 9. Governor May Fill Certain Vacancies

When any State or district office shall become vacant, and no mode is provided by the Constitution and laws for filling such vacancy, the Governor shall have the power to fill the same by granting a commission, which shall expire at the next election, and upon qualification of the person elected to such office.

Section 10. Governor's Appointive Power/Governor to Appoint to Fill Vacancy in other State Offices/Vacancy in the Office of the Lieutenant Governor

(1)
(a) The Governor shall nominate, and by and with consent of the Senate, appoint all State and district officers whose offices are established by this Constitution, or which may be created by law, and whose appointment or election is not otherwise provided for.

(b) If, during the recess of the Senate, a vacancy occurs in any State or district office, the Governor shall appoint some qualified person to discharge the duties thereof until the next meeting of the Senate, when the Governor shall nominate some person to fill such office.

(2) If the office of State Auditor, State Treasurer, or Attorney General be vacated by death, resignation, or otherwise, it shall be the duty of the Governor to fill the same by appointment, from the same political party as the removed person; and the appointee shall hold office until a successor shall be elected and qualified, as provided by law.

(3)
(a) A vacancy in the office of Lieutenant Governor occurs when:

(i) the Lieutenant Governor dies, resigns, is removed from office following impeachment, becomes Governor under Article VII, Section 11, ceases to reside within the State, or is determined, as provided in Subsection (3)(b), to have a disability that renders the Lieutenant Governor unable to discharge the duties of office for the remainder of the Lieutenant Governor's term of office; or

(ii) the Lieutenant Governor-elect fails to take office because of the Lieutenant Governor-elect's death, failure to qualify for office, or disability, determined as provided in Subsection (3)(b), that renders the Lieutenant Governor-elect unable to discharge the duties of office for the Lieutenant Governor-elect's full term of office.

(b)
(i) Except when the disability of a Lieutenant Governor is determined under Article VII, Section 11, Subsection (6) because the Lieutenant Governor is acting as Governor under Article VII, Section 11, Subsection (5), the disability of a Lieutenant Governor or Lieutenant Governor-elect shall be determined by a written declaration stating that the Lieutenant Governor or Lieutenant Governor-elect is unable to discharge the powers and

duties of the office.

(ii) The written declaration under Subsection (3)(b)(i) shall be transmitted to the Supreme Court and shall be signed by:

(A) the Governor; or

(B) (I) the Lieutenant Governor, if the Lieutenant Governor is the subject of the declaration; or

(II) the Lieutenant Governor-elect, if the Lieutenant Governor-elect is the subject of the declaration.

(iii) If the Lieutenant Governor or Lieutenant Governor-elect, as the case may be, disputes a declaration transmitted by the Governor under Subsection (3)(b)(i), the Lieutenant Governor or Lieutenant Governor-elect may, within ten days after the declaration is transmitted to the Supreme Court, file a petition requesting the Supreme Court to determine whether a disability exists as stated in the Governor's declaration.

(iv) In determining whether a disability exists, the Supreme Court shall follow procedures that the Court establishes, unless the Legislature by statute establishes procedures for the Supreme Court to follow in determining whether a disability exists.

(v) A determination of disability under this Subsection (3)(b) is final and conclusive.

(c)
(i) If a vacancy in the office of Lieutenant Governor occurs, the Governor shall, with the consent of the Senate, appoint a person as Lieutenant Governor, to serve:

(A) except as provided in Subsection (3)(c)(i)(B), the remainder of the unexpired term; or

(B) until the first Monday in January of the year following the next regular general election after the vacancy occurs, if an election is held for Governor and Lieutenant Governor under Article VII, Section 11, Subsection (4).

(ii) The person appointed as Lieutenant Governor under Subsection (3)(c)(i) shall be from the same political party as the Governor.

(iii) Neither the President of the Senate nor the Speaker of the House of Representatives may, while acting as Governor under Article VII, Section 11, Subsection (5), appoint a person as Lieutenant Governor to fill a vacancy in that office.

Section 11. Vacancy in Office of Governor/Determination of Disability

(1) A vacancy in the office of Governor occurs when:

(a) the Governor dies, resigns, is removed from office following impeachment, ceases to reside within the state, or is determined, as provided in Subsection (6), to have a disability that renders the Governor unable to discharge the duties of office for the remainder of the Governor's term of office; or

(b) the Governor-elect fails to take office because of the Governor-elect's death, failure to qualify for office, or disability, determined as provided in Subsection (6), that renders the Governor-elect unable to discharge the duties of office for the Governor-elect's full term of office.

(2) If a vacancy in the office of Governor occurs, the Lieutenant Governor shall become Governor, to serve:

(a) until the first Monday in January of the year following the next regular general election after the vacancy occurs, if the vacancy occurs during the first year of the term of office; or

(b) for the remainder of the unexpired term, if the vacancy occurs after the first year of the term of office.

(3) (a) In the event of simultaneous vacancies in the offices of Governor and Lieutenant Governor, the President of the Senate shall become Governor, to serve:

(i) until the first Monday in January of the year following the next regular general election after the vacancy occurs, if the vacancy occurs during the first year of the term of office; or

(ii) for the remainder of the unexpired term, if the vacancy occurs after the first year of the term of office.

(b) In the event of simultaneous vacancies in the offices of Governor, Lieutenant Governor, and President of the Senate, the Speaker of the House of Representatives shall become Governor, to serve:

(i) until the first Monday in January of the year following the next regular general election after the vacancy occurs, if the vacancy occurs during the first year of the term of office; or

(ii) for the remainder of the unexpired term, if the vacancy occurs after the first year of the term of office.

(4) If a vacancy in the office of Governor occurs during the first year of the term of office, an election shall be held at the next regular general election after the vacancy occurs to elect a Governor and Lieutenant Governor, as provided in Article VII, Section 2, to serve the remainder of the unexpired term.

(5)
(a) If the Governor is temporarily unable to discharge the duties of the office because of the Governor's temporary disability, as determined under Subsection (6), or if the Governor-elect is temporarily unable to assume the office of Governor because of the Governor-elect's temporary disability, as determined under

Subsection (6), the powers and duties of the Governor shall be discharged by the Lieutenant Governor who, in addition to discharging the duties of the office of Lieutenant Governor, shall, without additional compensation, act as Governor until the disability ceases.

(b) (i) If, during a temporary disability of the Governor or Governor-elect, as determined under Subsection (6), a vacancy in the office of Lieutenant Governor occurs or the Lieutenant Governor is temporarily unable to discharge the duties of the office of Governor because of the Lieutenant Governor's temporary disability, as determined under Subsection (6), the powers and duties of the Governor shall be discharged by the President of the Senate who shall act as Governor until the Governor or Governor-elect's disability ceases or, in the case of the Lieutenant Governor's temporary disability, the Lieutenant Governor's disability ceases, whichever occurs first.

(ii) If, during a temporary disability of the Governor or Governor-elect, as determined under Subsection (6), neither the Lieutenant Governor nor the President of the Senate is able to discharge the duties of the office of Governor because of a vacancy in the office of Lieutenant Governor or President of the Senate, or both, or because of a temporary disability of either or both officers, as determined under Subsection (6), or a combination of vacancy and temporary disability, the powers and duties of the Governor shall be discharged by the Speaker of the House of Representatives who shall act as Governor until the Governor's disability ceases or until the vacancy, if applicable, in the office of President of the Senate is filled or the temporary disability, if applicable, of the Lieutenant Governor or President of the Senate ceases, whichever occurs first.

(c) (i) During the time that the President of the Senate acts as Governor under this Subsection (5), the President may not exercise the powers and duties of President of the Senate or Senator. The powers and duties of President of the Senate may be exercised during that time by an acting President, chosen by the Senate.

(ii) During the time that the Speaker of the House of Representatives acts as Governor under this Subsection (5), the Speaker may not exercise the powers and duties of Speaker of the House of Representatives or Representative. The powers and duties of Speaker of the House of Representatives may be exercised during that time by an acting Speaker, chosen by the House of Representatives.

(d) When acting as Governor under this Subsection (5), the President of the Senate or Speaker of the House of Representatives, as the case may be, shall be entitled to receive the salary and emoluments of the office of Governor.

(6) (a) A disability of the Governor, Governor-elect, or person acting as Governor shall be determined by:

(i) the written declaration of the Governor, Governor-elect, or person acting as Governor, transmitted to the Supreme Court, stating an inability to discharge the powers and duties of the office; or

(ii) a majority of the Supreme Court upon the joint request of the President or, if applicable, acting President of the Senate and the Speaker or, if applicable, acting Speaker of the House of Representatives.

(b) The Governor or person acting as Governor shall resume or, in the case of a Governor-elect, shall assume the powers and duties of the office following a temporary disability upon the written declaration of the Governor, Governor-elect, or person acting as Governor, transmitted to the Supreme Court, that no disability exists, unless the Supreme Court, upon the joint request of the President or, if applicable, acting President of the Senate and the Speaker or, if applicable, acting Speaker of the House of Representatives, or upon its own initiative, determines that the temporary disability continues and that the Governor,

Governor-elect, or person acting as Governor is unable to discharge the powers and duties of the office.

(c) Each determination of a disability under Subsection (6)(a) shall be final and conclusive.

(7) The Supreme Court has exclusive jurisdiction to determine all questions arising under this section.

Section 12. Board of Pardons and Parole/Appointment/Powers and Procedures/Governor's Powers and Duties/Legislature's Powers

(1) There is created a Board of Pardons and Parole. The Governor shall appoint the members of the board with the consent of the Senate. The terms of office shall be as provided by statute.

(2) (a) The Board of Pardons and Parole, by majority vote and upon other conditions as provided by statute, may grant parole, remit fines, forfeitures, and restitution orders, commute punishments, and grant pardons after convictions, in all cases except treason and impeachments, subject to regulations as provided by statute.

(b) A fine, forfeiture, or restitution order may not be remitted and a commutation, parole, or pardon may not be granted except after a full hearing before the board, in open session, and after previous notice of the time and place of the hearing has been given.

(c) The proceedings and decisions of the board, the reasons therefor in each case, and the dissent of any member who may disagree shall be recorded and filed as provided by statute with all papers used upon the hearing.

(3) (a) The Governor may grant respites or reprieves in all cases of convictions for offenses against the state except treason or conviction on impeachment. These respites or reprieves may not extend beyond the next session of the board. At that session, the board shall continue or determine the respite or reprieve, commute the punishment, or pardon the offense as provided in this section.

(b) In case of conviction for treason, the Governor may suspend execution of the sentence until the case is reported to the Legislature at its next annual general session, when the Legislature shall pardon or commute the sentence, or direct its execution. If the Legislature takes no action on the case before adjournment of that session, the sentence shall be executed.

Section 14. Duties of Lieutenant Governor

The Lieutenant Governor shall:

(1) serve on all boards and commissions in lieu of the Governor whenever so designated by the Governor;

(2) perform such duties as may be delegated by the Governor; and

(3) perform other duties as may be provided by statute.

Section 15. Duties of State Auditor and State Treasurer.

(1) The State Auditor shall perform financial post audits of public accounts except as otherwise provided by this Constitution.

(2) The State Treasurer shall be the custodian of public moneys.

(3) Each shall perform other duties as provided by statute.

Section 16. Duties of Attorney General

The Attorney General shall be the legal adviser of the State officers, except as otherwise provided by this Constitution, and shall perform such other duties as provided by law.

Section 18. Compensation of State and Local Officers

(1) The Governor, Lieutenant Governor, State Auditor, State Treasurer, Attorney General, and any other state officer as the Legislature may provide, shall receive for their services a fixed and definite compensation as provided by law.

(2) (a) The compensation provided for in Subsection (1) shall be in full for all services rendered by those officers in any official capacity or employment during their terms of office.

(b) An officer may not receive for the performance of any official duty any fee for personal use, but all fees fixed by the Legislature for the performance by any of them of any official duty shall be collected in advance and deposited with the appropriate treasury.

(c) The Legislature may provide for the payment of actual and necessary expenses of those officers while traveling in the performance of official duties.

Section 19. Grants and Commissions

All grants and commissions shall be in the name and by the authority of the State of Utah, sealed with the Great Seal of the State, signed by the Governor, and countersigned by such officer as provided by law.

Section 20. The Great Seal

There shall be a seal of the State, which shall be called "The Great Seal of the State of Utah," and shall be kept by such officer as provided by law.

Section 21. United States Officials Ineligible to Hold State Office

No person, while holding any office under the United States government, shall hold any office under the State government of Utah.

ARTICLE VIII: JUDICIAL DEPARTMENT

Section 1. Judicial Powers/Courts

The judicial power of the state shall be vested in a Supreme Court, in a trial court of general jurisdiction known as the district court, and in such other courts as the Legislature by statute may establish. The Supreme Court, the district court, and such other courts designated by statute shall be courts of record. Courts not of record shall also be established by statute.

Section 2. Supreme Court/Chief Justice/Declaring Law Unconstitutional/Justice Unable to Participate

The Supreme Court shall be the highest court and shall consist of at least five justices. The number of justices may be changed by statute, but no change shall have the effect of removing a justice from office. A chief justice shall be selected from among the justices of the Supreme Court as provided by statute. The chief justice may resign as chief justice without resigning from the Supreme Court. The Supreme Court by rule may sit and render final judgment either en banc or in divisions. The court shall not declare any law unconstitutional under this constitution or the Constitution of the United States, except on the concurrence of a majority of all justices of the Supreme Court. If a justice of the Supreme Court is disqualified or otherwise unable to participate in a cause before the court, the chief justice, or in the event the chief justice is disqualified or unable to participate, the remaining justices, shall call an active judge from an appellate court or the district court to participate in the cause.

Section 3. Jurisdiction of Supreme Court

The Supreme Court shall have original jurisdiction to issue all extraordinary writs and to answer questions of state law certified by a court of the United States. The Supreme Court shall have appellate jurisdiction over all other matters to be exercised as provided by statute, and power to issue all writs and orders necessary for the exercise of the Supreme Court's jurisdiction or the complete determination of any cause.

Section 4. Rule-Making Power of Supreme Court/Judges Pro Tempore/Regulation of Practice of Law

The Supreme Court shall adopt rules of procedure and evidence to be used in the courts of the state and shall by rule manage the appellate process. The Legislature may amend the Rules of Procedure and Evidence adopted by the Supreme Court upon a vote of two-thirds of all members of both houses of the Legislature. Except as otherwise provided by this constitution, the Supreme Court by rule may authorize retired justices and judges and judges pro tempore to perform any judicial duties. Judges pro tempore shall be citizens of the United States, Utah residents, and admitted to practice law in Utah. The Supreme Court by rule shall govern the practice of law, including admission to practice law and the conduct and discipline of persons admitted to practice law.

Section 5. Jurisdiction of District Court and Other Courts/Right of Appeal

The district court shall have original jurisdiction in all matters except as limited by this constitution or by statute, and power to issue all extraordinary writs. The district court shall have appellate jurisdiction as provided by statute. The jurisdiction of all other courts, both original and appellate, shall be provided by statute. Except for matters filed originally with the Supreme Court, there shall be in all cases an appeal of right from the court of original jurisdiction to a court with appellate jurisdiction over the cause.

Section 6. Number Of Judges of District Court and Other Courts/Divisions

The number of judges of the district court and of other courts of record established by the Legislature shall be provided by statute. No change in the number of judges shall have the effect of removing a judge from office during a judge's term of office. Geographic divisions for all courts of record except the Supreme Court may be provided by statute. No change in divisions shall have the effect of removing a judge from office during a judge's term of office.

Section 7. Qualifications of Justices and Judges

Supreme court justices shall be at least 30 years old, United States citizens, Utah residents for five years preceding selection, and admitted to practice law in Utah. Judges of other courts of record shall be at least 25 years old, United States citizens, Utah residents for three years preceding selection, and admitted to practice law in Utah. If geographic divisions are provided for any court, judges of that court shall reside in the geographic division for which they are selected.

Section 8. Vacancies/Nominating Commissions/Senate Approval

(1) When a vacancy occurs in a court of record, the governor shall fill the vacancy by appointment from a list of at least three nominees certified to the governor by the Judicial Nominating Commission having authority over the vacancy. The governor shall fill the vacancy within 30 days after receiving the list of nominees. If the governor fails to fill the vacancy within the time prescribed, the chief justice of the Supreme Court shall within 20 days make the appointment from the list of nominees.

(2) The Legislature by statute shall provide for the nominating commissions' composition and procedures. No member of the Legislature may serve as a member of, nor may the Legislature appoint members to, any Judicial Nominating Commission.

(3) The Senate shall consider and render a decision on each judicial appointment within 60 days of the date of appointment. If necessary, the Senate shall convene itself in extraordinary session for the purpose of considering judicial appointments. The appointment shall be effective upon approval of a majority of all members of the Senate. If the Senate fails to approve the appointment, the office shall be considered vacant and a new nominating process shall commence.

(4) Selection of judges shall be based solely upon consideration of fitness for office without regard to any partisan political consideration.

Section 9. Judicial Retention Elections

Each appointee to a court of record shall be subject to an unopposed retention election at the first general election held more than three years after appointment. Following initial voter approval, each Supreme Court justice every tenth year, and each judge of other courts of record every sixth year, shall be subject to an unopposed retention election at the corresponding general election. Judicial retention elections shall be held on a nonpartisan ballot in a manner provided by statute. If geographic divisions are provided for any court of record, the judges of those courts shall stand for retention election only in the geographic division to which they are selected.

Section 10. Restrictions on Justices and Judges

Supreme court justices, district court judges, and judges of all other courts of record while holding office may not practice law, hold any elective nonjudicial public office, or hold office in a political party.

Section 11. Judges of Courts not of Record

Judges of courts not of record shall be selected in a manner, for a term, and with qualifications provided by statute. However, no qualification may be imposed which requires judges of courts not of record to be admitted to practice law. The number of judges of courts not of record shall be provided by statute.

Section 12. Judicial Council/Chief Justice as Administrative Officer/Legal Counsel

(1) There is created a Judicial Council which shall adopt rules for the administration of the courts of the state.

(2) The Judicial Council shall consist of the chief justice of the Supreme Court, as presiding officer, and other justices, judges, and other persons as provided by statute. There shall be at least one representative on the Judicial Council from each court established by the Constitution or by statute.

(3) The chief justice of the Supreme Court shall be the chief administrative officer for the courts and shall implement the rules adopted by the Judicial Council.

(4) The Judicial Council may appoint legal counsel which shall provide all legal services for the Judicial Department unless otherwise provided by statute.

Section 13. Judicial Conduct Commission

A Judicial Conduct Commission is established which shall investigate and conduct confidential hearings regarding complaints against any justice or judge. Following its investigations and hearings, the Judicial Conduct Commission may order the reprimand, censure, suspension, removal, or involuntary retirement of any justice or judge for the following:
(1) action which constitutes willful misconduct in office;

(2) final conviction of a crime punishable as a felony under state or federal law;

(3) willful and persistent failure to perform judicial duties;

(4) disability that seriously interferes with the performance of judicial duties; or

(5) conduct prejudicial to the administration of justice which brings a judicial office into disrepute.

Prior to the implementation of any commission order, the Supreme Court shall review the commission's proceedings as to both law and fact. The court may also permit the introduction of additional evidence. After its review, the Supreme Court shall, as it finds just and proper, issue its order implementing, rejecting, or modifying the commission's order. The Legislature by statute shall provide for the composition and procedures of the Judicial Conduct Commission.

Section 14. Compensation of Justices and Judges

The Legislature shall provide for the compensation of all justices and judges. The salaries of justices and judges shall not be diminished during their terms of office.

Section 15. Mandatory Retirement

The Legislature may provide standards for the mandatory retirement of justices and judges from office.

Section 16. Public Prosecutors

The Legislature shall provide for a system of public prosecutors who shall have primary responsibility for the prosecution of criminal actions brought in the name of the State of Utah and shall perform such other duties as may be provided by statute. Public prosecutors shall be elected in a manner provided by statute, and shall be admitted to practice law in Utah. If a public prosecutor fails or refuses to prosecute, the Supreme Court shall have power to appoint a prosecutor pro tempore.

ARTICLE IX: CONGRESSIONAL AND LEGISLATIVE APPORTIONMENT

Section 1. Dividing the State into Districts

No later than the annual general session next following the Legislature's receipt of the results of an enumeration made by the authority of the United States, the Legislature shall divide the state into congressional, legislative, and other districts accordingly.

Section 2. Number of Members of Legislature

The Senate shall consist of a membership not to exceed twenty-nine in number, and the number of representatives shall never be less than twice nor greater than three times the number of senators.

ARTICLE X: EDUCATION

Section 1. Free Nonsectarian Schools

The Legislature shall provide for the establishment and maintenance of the state's education systems including:

(a) a public education system, which shall be open to all children of the state; and

(b) a higher education system. Both systems shall be free from sectarian control.

Section 2. Defining What Shall Constitute the Public School System

The public education system shall include all public elementary and secondary schools and such other schools and programs as the Legislature may designate. The higher education system shall include all public universities and colleges and such other institutions and programs as the Legislature may designate. Public elementary and secondary schools shall be free, except the Legislature may authorize the imposition of fees in the secondary schools.

Section 3. State Board of Education

The general control and supervision of the public education system shall be vested in a State Board of Education. The membership of the board shall be established and elected as provided by statute. The State Board of Education shall appoint a State Superintendent of Public Instruction who shall be the executive officer of the board.

Section 4. Control of Higher Education System by Statute/Rights and Immunities Confirmed

The general control and supervision of the higher education system shall be provided for by statute. All rights, immunities, franchises, and endowments originally established or recognized by the constitution for any public university or college are confirmed.

Section 5. State School Fund and Uniform School Fund/Establishment and Use/Debt Guaranty

(1) There is established a permanent State School Fund which consists of:

(a) proceeds from the sales of all lands granted by the United States to this state for the support of the public elementary and secondary schools;

(b) 5% of the net proceeds from the sales of United States public lands lying within this state;

(c) all revenues derived from nonrenewable resources on state lands, other than sovereign lands and lands granted for other specific purposes;

(d) all revenues derived from the use of school trust lands;

(e) revenues appropriated by the Legislature; and

(f) other revenues and assets received by the permanent State School Fund under any other provision of law or by bequest or donation.

(2)
(a) The permanent State School Fund shall be prudently invested by the state and shall be held by the state in perpetuity.

(b) Only earnings received from investment of the permanent State School Fund may be distributed from the fund, and any distribution from the fund shall be for the support of the public education system as defined in Article X, Section 2 of this constitution.

(c) Annual distributions from the permanent State School Fund under Subsection (2)(b) may not exceed 4% of the fund, calculated as provided by statute.

(d) The Legislature may make appropriations from school trust land revenues to provide funding necessary for the proper administration and management of those lands consistent with the state's fiduciary responsibilities towards the beneficiaries of the school land trust. Unexpended balances remaining from the appropriation at the end of each fiscal year shall be deposited in the permanent State School Fund.

(e) The permanent State School Fund shall be guaranteed by the state against loss or diversion.

(3) There is established a Uniform School Fund which consists of:

(a) money from the permanent State School Fund;

(b) revenues appropriated by the Legislature; and

(c) other revenues received by the Uniform School Fund under any other provision of law or by donation.

(4) The Uniform School Fund shall be maintained and used for the support of the state's public education system as defined in Article X, Section 2 of this constitution and apportioned as the Legislature shall provide.

(5)
(a) Notwithstanding Article VI, Section 29, the State may guarantee the debt of school districts created in accordance with Article XIV, Section 3, and may guarantee debt incurred to refund the school district debt. Any debt guaranty, the school district debt guaranteed thereby, or any borrowing of the state undertaken to facilitate the payment of the state's obligation under any debt guaranty shall not be included as a debt of the state for purposes of the 1.5% limitation of Article XIV, Section 1.

(b) The Legislature may provide that reimbursement to the state shall be obtained from monies which otherwise would be used for the support of the educational programs of the school district which incurred the debt with respect to which a payment under the state's guaranty was made.

Section 7. Proceeds of Land Grants Constitute Permanent Funds

The proceeds from the sale of lands reserved by Acts of Congress for the establishment or benefit of the state's universities and colleges shall constitute permanent funds to be used for the purposes for which the funds were established. The funds' principal shall be safely invested and held by the state in perpetuity. Any income from the funds shall be used exclusively for the support and maintenance of the respective universities and colleges. The Legislature by statute may provide for necessary administrative costs. The funds shall be guaranteed by the state against loss or diversion.

Section 8. No Religious or Partisan Tests in Schools

No religious or partisan test or qualification shall be required as a condition of employment, admission, or attendance in the state's education systems.

Section 9. Public Aid to Church Schools Forbidden

Neither the state of Utah nor its political subdivisions may make any appropriation for the direct support of any school or educational institution controlled by any religious organization.

ARTICLE XI: COUNTIES, CITIES AND TOWNS

Section 1. Counties Recognized as Legal Subdivisions

The counties of the State of Utah are recognized as legal subdivisions of this State. The counties now existing shall continue until changed as provided by statute.

Section 2. Moving a County Seat

A county seat may be moved only when at a countywide general election two-thirds of those voting on the proposition vote in favor of moving the county seat. A proposition to move the county seat may not be submitted in the same county more than once in four years.

Section 3. Changing County Lines

(1) Except as provided in Subsection (2), no territory may be stricken from any county unless a majority of the voters living in that county who vote on the proposition, as well as a majority of the voters living in the county to which it is to be annexed who vote on the proposition, shall vote therefore, and then only under such conditions as may be prescribed by general law.

(2) Counties sharing a common boundary may, through their county legislative bodies, make a minor adjustment, as defined by statute, to the common boundary.

Section 4. Optional Forms of County Government

The Legislature shall by statute provide for optional forms of county government. The selection of an optional form shall be subject to voter approval as provided by statute.

Section 5. Cities and Towns not to be Created by Special Laws/Legislature to Provide for the Incorporation, Organization, Dissolution, and Classification of Cities and Towns/Charter Cities

The Legislature may not create cities or towns by special laws. The Legislature by statute shall provide for the incorporation, organization, and dissolution of cities and towns and for their classification in proportion to population. Any incorporated city or town may frame and adopt a charter for its own government in the following manner:

The legislative authority of the city may, by two-thirds vote of its members, and upon petition of qualified electors to the number of fifteen per cent of all votes cast at the next preceding election for the office of the mayor, shall forthwith provide by ordinance for the submission to the electors of the question:

"Shall a commission be chosen to frame a charter?"

The ordinance shall require that the question be submitted to the electors at the next regular municipal election. The ballot containing such question shall also contain the names of candidates for members of the proposed commission, but without party designation. Such candidates shall be nominated in the same manner as required by law for nomination of city officers. If a majority of the electors voting on the question of choosing a commission shall vote in the affirmative, then the fifteen candidates receiving a majority of the votes cast at such election, shall constitute the charter commission, and shall proceed to frame a charter.

Any charter so framed shall be submitted to the qualified electors of the city at an election to be held at a time to be determined by the charter commission, which shall be not less than sixty days subsequent to its completion and distribution among the electors and not more than one year from such date. Alternative provisions may also be submitted to be voted upon separately. The commission shall make provisions for the distribution of copies of the proposed charter and of any alternative provisions to the qualified electors of the city, not less than sixty days before the election at which it is voted upon. Such proposed charter and such alternative provisions as are approved by a majority of the electors voting thereon, shall become an organic law of such city at such time as may be fixed therein, and shall supersede any existing charter and all laws affecting the organization and government of such city which are now in conflict therewith. Within thirty days after its approval a copy of such charter as adopted, certified by the mayor and city recorder and authenticated by the seal of such city, shall be made in duplicate and deposited, one in the office of the secretary of State and the other in the office of the city recorder, and thereafter all courts shall take judicial notice of such charter. Amendments to any such charter may be framed and submitted by a charter commission in the same manner as provided for making of charters, or may be proposed by the legislative authority of the city upon a two-thirds vote thereof, or by petition of qualified electors to a number equal to fifteen per cent of the total votes cast for mayor on the next preceding election, and any such amendment may be submitted at the next regular municipal election, and having been approved by the majority of the electors voting thereon, shall become part of the charter at the time fixed in such amendment and shall be certified and filed as provided in case of charters.

Each city forming its charter under this section shall have, and is hereby granted, the authority to exercise all powers relating to municipal affairs, and to adopt and enforce within its limits, local police, sanitary and similar regulations not in conflict with the general law, and no enumeration of powers in this constitution or any law shall be deemed to limit or restrict the general grant of authority hereby conferred; but this grant of authority shall not include the power to regulate public utilities, not municipally owned, if any such regulation of public utilities is provided for by general law, nor be deemed to limit or restrict the power of the Legislature in matters relating to State affairs, to enact general laws applicable alike to all cities of the State.

The power to be conferred upon the cities by this section shall include the following:

(a) To levy, assess and collect taxes and borrow money, within the limits prescribed by general law, and to levy and collect special assessments for benefits conferred.

(b) To furnish all local public services, to purchase, hire, construct, own, maintain and operate, or lease, public utilities local in extent and use; to acquire by condemnation, or otherwise, within or without the corporate limits, property necessary for any such purposes, subject to restrictions imposed by general law for the protection of other communities; and to grant local public utility franchises and within its powers regulate the exercise thereof.

(c) To make local public improvements and to acquire by condemnation, or otherwise, property within its corporate limits necessary for such improvements; and also to acquire an excess over than [that] needed for any such improvement and to sell or lease such excess property with restrictions, in order to protect and preserve the improvement.

(d) To issue and sell bonds on the security of any such excess property, or of any public utility owned by the city, or of the revenues thereof, or both, including, in the case of public utility, a franchise stating the terms upon which, in case of foreclosure, the purchaser may operate such utility.

Section 6. Municipalities Forbidden to Sell Waterworks or Rights

No municipal corporation, shall directly or indirectly, lease, sell, alien or dispose of any waterworks, water rights, or sources of water supply now, or hereafter to be owned or controlled by it; but all such waterworks, water rights and sources of water supply now owned or hereafter to be acquired by any municipal corporation, shall be preserved, maintained and operated by it for supplying its inhabitants with water at reasonable charges:

Provided, That nothing herein contained shall be construed to prevent any such municipal corporation from exchanging water-rights, or sources of water supply, for other water-rights or sources of water supply of equal value, and to be devoted in like manner to the public supply of its inhabitants.

Section 7. Special Service Districts

(1) The Legislature may by statute authorize:

(a) a county, city, or town to establish a special service district within all or any part of the county, city, or town, to be governed by the governing authority of the county, city, or town, and to provide services as provided by statute;

(b) a county, city, or town to levy taxes upon the taxable property in the special service district for the purpose of acquiring, constructing, equipping, operating, and maintaining facilities required for any or all of the services the special service district is authorized to provide; and

(c) a special service district to issue bonds of the special service district for the purpose of acquiring, constructing, and equipping any of the facilities required for any or all of the services the special service district is authorized to provide, without regard to the limitations of Article XIV, Sections 3 and 4, but subject to such limitation on the aggregate amount of the bonds outstanding at any one time as may be provided by statute.

(2) The authority to levy taxes upon the taxable property in a special service district and to issue bonds payable from taxes levied on the taxable property in the special service district shall be conditioned upon the assent of a majority of the qualified electors of the special service district voting in an election for this purpose to be held as provided by statute.

(3) A special service district created by a county may contain all or part of one or more cities or towns, but only with the consent of the governing authority of each city or town to be included in the special service district.

Section 8. Political Subdivisions of the State or other Governmental Entities in Addition to Counties, Cities, Towns, School Districts, and Special Service Districts

The Legislature may by statute provide for the establishment of political subdivisions of the State, or other governmental entities, in addition to counties, cities, towns, school districts, and special service districts, to provide services and facilities as provided by statute. Those other political subdivisions of the State or other governmental entities may exercise those powers and perform those functions that are provided by statute.

Section 9. Consent of Local Authorities Necessary for use of Streets

The Legislature may not grant the right to construct and operate a street railroad, telegraph, telephone, or electric light plant within a city or town without the consent of the local authorities who have control of the street or highway proposed to be occupied for such purposes.

ARTICLE XII: CORPORATIONS

Section 1. Corporations Formation

Corporations may be formed under general laws but may not be created by special acts.

Section 4. Suits

All corporations may sue and be sued, in all courts, in like cases as natural persons.

Section 12. Common Carriers/No Discrimination

All common carriers shall provide services without discrimination.

Section 19. Blacklisting Forbidden

Each person in Utah is free to obtain and enjoy employment whenever possible, and a person or corporation, or their agent, servant, or employee may not maliciously interfere with any person from obtaining employment or enjoying employment already obtained from any other person or corporation.

Section 20. Free Market System as State Policy/Restraint of Trade and Monopolies Prohibited

It is the policy of the state of Utah that a free market system shall govern trade and commerce in this state to promote the dispersion of economic and political power and the general welfare of all the people. Each contract, combination in the form of trust or otherwise, or conspiracy in restraint of trade or commerce is prohibited. Except as otherwise provided by statute, it is also prohibited for any person to monopolize, attempt to monopolize, or combine or conspire with any other person or persons to monopolize any part of trade or commerce.

ARTICLE XIII: REVENUE AND TAXATION

Section 1. Fiscal Year

The Legislature shall by statute establish the fiscal year of the State.

Section 2. Property Tax

(1) So that each person and corporation pays a tax in proportion to the fair market value of his, her, or its tangible property, all tangible property in the State that is not exempt under the laws of the United States or under this Constitution shall be:

(a) assessed at a uniform and equal rate in proportion to its fair market value, to be ascertained as provided by law; and

(b) taxed at a uniform and equal rate.

(2) Each corporation and person in the State or doing business in the State is subject to taxation on the tangible property owned or used by the corporation or person within the boundaries of the State or local authority levying the tax.

(3) The Legislature may provide by statute that land used for agricultural purposes be assessed based on its value for agricultural use.

(4) The Legislature may by statute determine the manner and extent of taxing livestock.

(5) The Legislature may by statute determine the manner and extent of taxing or exempting intangible property, except that any property tax on intangible property may not exceed .005 of its fair market value. If any intangible property is taxed under the property tax, the income from that property may not also be taxed.

(6) Tangible personal property required by law to be registered with the State before it is used on a public highway or waterway, on public land, or in the air may be exempted from property tax by statute. If the Legislature exempts tangible personal property from property tax under this Subsection (6), it shall provide for the payment of uniform statewide fees or uniform statewide rates of assessment or taxation on that property in lieu of the property tax. The fair market value of any property exempted under this Subsection (6) shall be considered part of the State tax base for determining the debt limitation under Article XIV.

Section 3. Property Tax Exemptions

(1) The following are exempt from property tax:

(a) property owned by the State;

(b) property owned by a public library;

(c) property owned by a school district;

(d) property owned by a political subdivision of the State, other than a school district, and located within the political subdivision;

(e) property owned by a political subdivision of the State, other than a school district, and located outside the political subdivision unless the Legislature by statute authorizes the property tax on that property;

(f) property owned by a nonprofit entity used exclusively for religious, charitable, or educational purposes;

(g) places of burial not held or used for private or corporate benefit;

(h) farm equipment and farm machinery as defined by statute;

(i) water rights, reservoirs, pumping plants, ditches, canals, pipes, flumes, power plants, and transmission lines to the extent owned and used by an individual or corporation to irrigate land that is:

(i) within the State; and

(ii) owned by the individual or corporation, or by an individual member of the corporation; and

(j) (i) if owned by a nonprofit entity and used within the State to irrigate land, provide domestic water, as defined by statute, or provide water to a public water supplier:
(A) water rights; and

(B) reservoirs, pumping plants, ditches, canals, pipes, flumes, and, as defined by statute, other water infrastructure;

(ii) land occupied by a reservoir, ditch, canal, or pipe that is exempt under Subsection (1)(j)(i)(B) if the land is owned by the nonprofit entity that owns the reservoir, ditch, canal, or pipe; and

(iii) land immediately adjacent to a reservoir, ditch, canal, or pipe that is exempt under Subsection (1)(j)(i)(B) if the land is:

(A) owned by the nonprofit entity that owns the adjacent reservoir, ditch, canal, or pipe; and

(B) reasonably necessary for the maintenance or for otherwise supporting the operation of the reservoir, ditch, canal, or pipe.

(2) (a) The Legislature may by statute exempt the following from property tax:

(i) tangible personal property constituting inventory present in the State on January 1 and held for sale in the ordinary course of business;

(ii) tangible personal property present in the State on January 1 and held for sale or processing and shipped to a final destination outside the State within 12 months;

(iii) subject to Subsection (2)(b), property to the extent used to generate and deliver electrical power for pumping water to irrigate lands in the State;

(iv) up to 45% of the fair market value of residential property, as defined by statute;

(v) household furnishings, furniture, and equipment used exclusively by the owner of that property in maintaining the owner's home; and

(vi) tangible personal property that, if subject to property tax, would generate an inconsequential amount of revenue.

(b) The exemption under Subsection (2)(a)(iii) shall accrue to the benefit of the users of pumped water as provided by statute.

(3) The following may be exempted from property tax as provided by statute:

(a) property owned by a disabled person who, during military training or a military conflict, was disabled in the line of duty in the military service of the United States or the State; and

(b) property owned by the unmarried surviving spouse or the minor orphan of a person who:

(i) is described in Subsection (3)(a); or

(ii) during military training or a military conflict, was killed in action or died in the line of duty in the military service of the United States or the State.

(c) real property owned by a person in the military or the person's spouse, or both, and used as the person's primary residence, if the person serves under an order to federal active duty out of state for at least 200 days in a calendar year or 200 consecutive days.

(4) The Legislature may by statute provide for the remission or abatement of the taxes of the poor.

Section 4. Other Taxes

(1) Nothing in this Constitution may be construed to prevent the Legislature from providing by statute for taxes other than the property tax and for deductions, exemptions, and offsets from those other taxes.

(2) In a statute imposing an income tax, the Legislature may:

(a) define the amount on which the tax is imposed by reference to a provision of the laws of the United States as from time to time amended; and

(b) modify or provide exemptions to a provision referred to in Subsection (2)(a).

Section 5. Use and Amount of Taxes and Expenditures

(1) The Legislature shall provide by statute for an annual tax sufficient, with other revenues, to defray the estimated ordinary expenses of the State for each fiscal year.

(2) (a) For any fiscal year, the Legislature may not make an appropriation or authorize an expenditure if the State's expenditure exceeds the total tax provided for by statute and applicable to the particular appropriation or expenditure.

(b) Subsection (2)(a) does not apply to an appropriation or expenditure to suppress insurrection, defend the State, or assist in defending the United States in time of war.

(3) For any debt of the State, the Legislature shall provide by statute for an annual tax sufficient to pay:

(a) the annual interest; and

(b) the principal within 20 years after the final passage of the statute creating the debt.

(4) Except as provided in Article X, Section 5, Subsection (5)(a), the Legislature may not impose a tax for the purpose of a political subdivision of the State, but may by statute authorize political subdivisions of the State to assess and collect taxes for their own purposes.

(5) All revenue from taxes on intangible property or from a tax on income shall be used to support the systems of public education and higher education as defined in Article X, Section 2.

(6) Proceeds from fees, taxes, and other charges related to the operation of motor vehicles on public highways and proceeds from an excise tax on liquid motor fuel used to propel those motor vehicles shall be used for:

(a) statutory refunds and adjustments and costs of collection and administration;

(b) the construction, maintenance, and repair of State and local roads, including payment for property taken for or damaged by rights-of-way and for associated administrative costs;

(c) driver education;

(d) enforcement of state motor vehicle and traffic laws; and

(e) the payment of the principal of and interest on any obligation of the State or a city or county, issued for any of the purposes set forth in Subsection (6)(b) and to which any of the fees, taxes, or other charges described in this Subsection (6) have been pledged, including any paid to the State or a city or county, as provided by statute.

(7) Fees and taxes on tangible personal property imposed under Section 2, Subsection (6) of this article are not subject to Subsection (6) of this Section 5 and shall be distributed to the taxing districts in which the property is located in the same proportion as that in which the revenue collected from real property tax is distributed.

(8) A political subdivision of the State may share its tax and other revenues with another political subdivision of the State as provided by statute.

(9) Beginning July 1, 2016, the aggregate annual revenue from all severance taxes, as those taxes are defined by statute, except revenue that by statute is used for purposes related to any federally recognized Indian tribe, shall be deposited annually into the permanent State trust fund under Article XXII, Section 4, as follows:

(a) 25% of the first $50,000,000 of aggregate annual revenue;

(b) 50% of the next $50,000,000 of aggregate annual revenue; and

(c) 75% of the aggregate annual revenue that exceeds $100,000,000.

Section 6. State Tax Commission

(1) There shall be a State Tax Commission consisting of four members, not more than two of whom may belong to the same political party.

(2) With the consent of the Senate, the Governor shall appoint the members of the State Tax Commission for such terms as may be provided by statute.

(3) The State Tax Commission shall:

(a) administer and supervise the State's tax laws;

(b) assess mines and public utilities and have such other powers of original assessment as the Legislature may provide by statute;

(c) adjust and equalize the valuation and assessment of property among the counties;

(d) as the Legislature provides by statute, review proposed bond issues, revise local tax levies, and equalize the assessment and valuation of property within the counties; and

(e) have other powers as may be provided by statute.

(4) Notwithstanding the powers granted to the State Tax Commission in this Constitution, the Legislature may by statute authorize any court established under Article VIII to adjudicate, review, reconsider, or redetermine any matter decided by the State Tax Commission relating to revenue and taxation.

Section 7. County Boards of Equalization

(1) In each county, there shall be a county board of equalization consisting of elected county officials as provided by statute.

(2) Each county board of equalization shall adjust and equalize the valuation and assessment of the real and personal property within its county, subject to the State Tax Commission's regulation and control as provided by law.

(3) The county boards of equalization shall have other powers as may be provided by statute.

(4) Notwithstanding the powers granted to the State Tax Commission in this Constitution, the Legislature may by statute authorize any court established under Article VIII to adjudicate, review, reconsider, or redetermine any matter decided by a county board of equalization relating to revenue and taxation.

Section 8. Annual Statement

The State shall publish annually an accurate statement of the receipt and expenditure of public money in a manner provided by statute.

ARTICLE XIV: PUBLIC DEBT

Section 1. Fixing the Limit of the State Indebtedness/Exceptions

To meet casual deficits or failures in revenue, and for necessary expenditures for public purposes, including the erection of public buildings, and for the payment of all Territorial indebtedness assumed by the State, the State may contract debts, not exceeding in the aggregate at any one time, an amount equal to one and one-half per centum of the value of the taxable property of the State, as shown by the last assessment for State purposes, previous to the incurring of such indebtedness. But the State shall never contract any indebtedness, except as provided in Article XIV, Section 2, in excess of such amount, and all monies arising from loans herein authorized, shall be applied solely to the purposes for which they were obtained.

Section 2. Debts for Public Defense

The State may contract debts to repel invasion, suppress insurrection, or to defend the State in war, but the money arising from the contracting of such debts shall be applied solely to the purpose for which it was obtained.

Section 3. Certain Debt of Counties, Cities, Towns, School Districts, and Other Political Subdivisions not to Exceed Taxes/Exception/Debt may be Incurred only for Specified Purposes

(1) No debt issued by a county, city, town, school district, or other political subdivision of the State and directly payable from and secured by ad valorem property taxes levied by the issuer of the debt may be created in excess of the taxes for the current year unless the proposition to create the debt has been submitted to a vote of qualified voters at the time and in the manner provided by statute, and a majority of those voting thereon has voted in favor of incurring the debt.

(2) No part of the indebtedness allowed in this section may be incurred for other than strictly county, city, town, school district, or other political subdivision purposes respectively.

Section 4. Limit of Indebtedness of Counties, Cities, Towns, and School Districts/Larger Indebtedness may be Allowed

(1) (a) If authorized to create indebtedness as provided in Section 3 of this Article, no county may become indebted to an amount, including existing indebtedness, exceeding two per centum of the value of taxable property in the county.

(b) No city, town, school district, or other municipal corporation, may become indebted to an amount, including existing indebtedness, exceeding four per centum of the value of the taxable property therein.

(2) For purposes of Subsection (1), the value of taxable property shall be ascertained by the last assessment for State and County purposes previous to the incurring of the indebtedness, except that in incorporated cities the assessment shall be taken from the last assessment for city purposes.

(3) A city of the first or second class, if authorized as provided in Section 3 of this Article, may be allowed to incur a larger indebtedness, not to exceed four per centum, and any other city or town, not to exceed eight per centum additional, for supplying such city or town with water, artificial lights or sewers, if the works for supplying the water, light, and sewers are owned and controlled by the municipality.

Section 5. Borrowed Money to be Applied to Authorized Use

All moneys borrowed by, or on behalf of the State or any legal subdivision thereof, shall be used solely for the purpose specified in the law authorizing the loan.

Section 6. State not to assume county, city, town or school district debts/Exception.

The State shall not assume the debt, or any part thereof, of any county, city, town or school district except as provided in Article X, Section 5.

Section 7. Existing Indebtedness Not Impaired

Nothing in this article shall be so construed as to impair or add to the obligation of any debt heretofore contracted, in accordance with the laws of Utah Territory, by any county, city, town or school district, or to prevent the contracting of any debt, or the issuing of bonds therefore, in accordance with said laws, upon any proposition for that purpose, which, according to said laws, may have been submitted to a vote of the qualified electors of any county, city, town or school district before the day on which this Constitution takes effect.

ARTICLE XV: MILITIA

Section 1. How Constituted

The militia shall consist of all able-bodied male inhabitants of the State, between the ages of eighteen and forty-five years, except such as are exempted by law.

Section 2. Organization and Equipment

The Legislature shall provide by law for the organization, equipment and discipline of the militia, which shall conform as nearly as practicable to the regulations for the government of the armies of the United States.

ARTICLE XVI: LABOR

Section 1. Rights of Labor to be Protected

The rights of labor shall have just protection through laws calculated to promote the industrial welfare of the State.

Section 2. Board of Labor

The Legislature shall provide by law, for a Board of Labor, Conciliation and Arbitration, which shall fairly represent the interests of both capital and labor. The Board shall perform duties, and receive compensation as prescribed by law.

Section 3. Certain Employment and Practices to be Prohibited

The Legislature shall prohibit:

(1) The employment of children under the age of fourteen years, in underground mines.

(2) The involuntary contracting of convict labor.

(3) The political and commercial control of employees.

Section 4. Exchange of Blacklists Prohibited

The exchange of black lists by railroad companies, or other corporations, associations or persons is prohibited.

Section 5. Injuries Resulting in Death/Damages

The right of action to recover damages for injuries resulting in death, shall never be abrogated, and the amount recoverable shall not be subject to any statutory limitation, except in cases where compensation for injuries resulting in death is provided for by law.

Section 6. Eight Hours a Day's Labor On Public Works/Health And Safety Laws

Eight hours shall constitute a day's work on all works or undertakings carried on or aided by the State, County or Municipal governments; and the Legislature shall pass laws to provide for the health and safety of employees in factories, smelters and mines.

Section 7. Legislature to Enforce this Article

The Legislature, by appropriate legislation, shall provide for the enforcement of the provisions of this article.

Section 8. Minimum Wage for Women and Minors/Comfort and Safety Laws

The legislature may, by appropriate legislation provide for the establishment of a minimum wage for women and minors and may provide for the comfort, safety and general welfare of any and all employees. No provision of this constitution shall be construed as a limitation upon the authority of the legislature to confer upon any commission now or hereafter created such power and authority as the legislature may deem requisite to carry out the provisions of this section.

ARTICLE XVII: WATER RIGHTS

Section 1. Existing Rights Confirmed

All existing rights to the use of any of the waters in this State for any useful or beneficial purpose, are hereby recognized and confirmed.

ARTICLE XVIII: FORESTRY

Section 1. Forests to be Preserved

The Legislature shall enact laws to prevent the destruction of and to preserve the Forests on the lands of the State, and upon any part of the public domain, the control of which may be conferred by Congress upon the State.

ARTICLE XX: PUBLIC LANDS

Section 1. Land Grants Accepted on Terms of Trust

All lands of the State that have been, or may hereafter be granted to the State by Congress, and all lands acquired by gift, grant or devise, from any person or corporation, or that may otherwise be acquired, are hereby accepted, and, except as provided in Section 2 of this Article, are declared to be the public lands of the State; and shall be held in trust for the people, to be disposed of as may be provided by law, for the respective purposes for which they have been or may be granted, donated, devised or otherwise acquired.

Section 2. School and Institutional Trust Lands

Lands granted to the State under Sections 6, 8, and 12 of the Utah Enabling Act, and other lands which may be added to those lands pursuant to those sections through purchase, exchange, or other means, are declared to be school and institutional trust lands, held in trust by the State for the respective beneficiaries and purposes stated in the Enabling Act grants.

ARTICLE XXII: MISCELLANEOUS

Section 1. Homestead Exemption

The Legislature shall provide by statute for an exemption of a homestead, which may consist of one or more parcels of lands, together with the appurtenances and improvements thereon, from sale on execution.

Section 2. Missing

Section 3. Seat of Government

The seat of state government shall be at Salt Lake City.

Section 4. State trust fund/Principal to be held in perpetuity/Use of income.

(1) There is established a permanent state trust fund consisting of:

(a) as provided by statute or appropriation, funds that the state receives relating to the November 1998 settlement agreement with leading tobacco manufacturers;

(b) money or other assets given to the fund under any provision of law;

(c) severance tax revenue, as provided in Article XIII, Section 5, Subsection (9); and

(d) other funds and assets that the trust fund receives by bequest or private donation.

(2) Except as provided in Subsection (4), the state treasurer shall, as provided by statute, hold all trust funds and assets in trust and invest them for the benefit of the people of the state in perpetuity.

(3) The income from the state trust fund shall be deposited into the General Fund.

(4) With the concurrence of the governor and three-fourths of each house of the Legislature, funds or assets in the trust fund may be removed from the fund for deposit into the General Fund.

Section 5. Officers May Not Profit

Each public officer who makes a profit from public money or uses public money for a purpose not authorized by law shall be guilty of a felony and shall be punished as provided by law, but part of the punishment shall be disqualification to hold public office.

ARTICLE XXIII: AMENDMENT AND REVISION

Section 1. Amendments: Proposal, Election

Any amendment or amendments to this Constitution may be proposed in either house of the Legislature, and if two-thirds of all the members elected to each of the two houses, shall vote in favor thereof, such proposed amendment or amendments shall be entered on their respective journals with the yeas and nays taken thereon; and the Legislature shall cause the same to be published in at least one newspaper in every county of the state, where a newspaper is published, for two months immediately preceding the next general election, at which time the said amendment or amendments shall be submitted to the electors of the state for their approval or rejection, and if a majority of the electors voting thereon shall approve the same, such amendment or amendments shall become part of this Constitution.
The revision or amendment of an entire article or the addition of a new article to this Constitution may be proposed as a single amendment and may be submitted to the electors as a single question or proposition. Such amendment may relate to one subject, or any number of subjects, and may modify, or repeal provisions contained in other articles of the Constitution, if such provisions are germane to the subject matter of the article being revised, amended or being proposed as a new article.

Section 2. Revision of the Constitution

Whenever two-thirds of the members, elected to each branch of the Legislature, shall deem it necessary to call a convention to revise or amend this Constitution, they shall recommend to the electors to vote, at the next general election, for or against a convention, and, if a majority of all the electors, voting at such election, shall vote for a convention, the Legislature, at its next session, shall provide by law for calling the same. The convention shall consist of not less than the number of members in both branches of the Legislature.

Section 3. Submission to Electors

No Constitution, or amendments adopted by such convention, shall have validity until submitted to, and adopted by, a majority of the electors of the State voting at the next general election.

ARTICLE XXIV: SCHEDULE

Section 1. Actions, Contracts to Continue

In order that no inconvenience may arise, by reason of the change from a Territorial to a State Government, it is hereby declared that all writs, actions, prosecutions, judgments, claims and contracts, as well of individuals as of bodies corporate, both public and private, shall continue as if no change had taken place; and all process which may issue, under the authority of the Territory of Utah, previous to its admission into the Union, shall be as valid as if issued in the name of the State of Utah.

Section 2. Territorial Laws Continued

All laws of the Territory of Utah now in force, not repugnant to this Constitution, shall remain in force until they expire by their own limitations, or are altered or repealed by the Legislature. The act of the Governor and Legislative Assembly of the Territory of Utah, entitled, "An Act to punish polygamy and other kindred offenses," approved February 4th, A.D. 1892, in so far as the same defines and imposes penalties for polygamy, is hereby declared to be in force in the State of Utah.

Section 3. Prisoners to be Held

Any person, who, at the time of the admission of the State into the Union, may be confined under lawful commitment, or otherwise lawfully held to answer for alleged violation of any of the criminal laws of the Territory of Utah, shall continue to be so held or confined, until discharged therefrom by the proper courts of the State.

Section 4. Fines, Penalties and Forfeitures Due the Territory/Debts of the Territory

All fines, penalties and forfeitures accruing to the people of the United States in the Territory of Utah, shall inure to this State, and all debts, liabilities and obligations of said Territory shall be valid against the State, and enforced as may be provided by law.

Section 5. Recognizances/Judgments/Records/Fines Due Counties, Municipalities and School Districts

All recognizances heretofore taken, or which may be taken before the change from a Territorial to a State Government, shall remain valid, and shall pass to and be prosecuted in the name of the State; and all bonds executed to the Governor of the Territory, or to any other officer or court in his or their official capacity, or to any official board for the benefit of the Territory of Utah, or the people thereof, shall pass to the Governor or other officer, court or board, and his or their successors in office, for the uses therein, respectively expressed, and may be sued on, and recovery had accordingly. Assessed taxes, and all revenue, property, real, personal or mixed, and all judgments, bonds, specialties, choses in action, claims and debts, of whatsoever description; and all records and public archives of the Territory of Utah, shall issue and vest in the State of Utah, and may be sued for and recovered, in the same manner, and to the same extent by the State of Utah, as the same could have been by the Territory of Utah; and all fines, taxes, penalties and forfeitures, due or owing to any county, municipality or school district therein, at the time the State shall be admitted into the Union, are hereby respectively assigned and transferred, and the same shall be payable to the county, municipality or school district, as the case may be, and payment thereof be enforced under the laws of the State.

Section 6. Criminal Prosecutions Begun and Crimes Committed Before Statehood

All criminal prosecutions, and penal actions, which may have arisen, or which may arise before the change from a Territorial to a State Government, and which shall then be pending, shall be prosecuted to judgment and execution in the name of the State, and in the court having jurisdiction thereof. All offenses committed against the laws of the Territory of Utah, before the change from a Territorial to a State Government, and which shall not have been prosecuted before such change, may be prosecuted in the name, and by authority of the State of Utah, with like effect as though such change had not taken place, and all penalties incurred shall remain the same, as if this Constitution had not been adopted.

Section 7. Transfer of Causes, Records

All actions, cases, proceedings and matters, pending in the Supreme and District Courts of the Territory of Utah, at the time the State shall be admitted into the Union, and all files, records and indictments relating thereto, except as otherwise provided herein, shall be appropriately transferred to the Supreme and District Courts of the State respectively; and thereafter all such actions, matters and cases, shall be proceeded with in the proper State courts. All actions, cases, proceedings and matters which shall be pending in the District Courts of the Territory of Utah, at the time of the admission of the State into the Union, whereof the United States Circuit or District Courts might have had jurisdiction had there been a State Government at the time of the commencement thereof respectively, shall be transferred to the proper United States Circuit and District Courts respectively; and all files, records, indictments and proceedings relating thereto, shall be transferred to said United States Courts: Provided, That no civil actions, other than causes and proceedings of which the said United States' Courts shall have exclusive jurisdiction, shall be transferred to either of said United States' Courts except upon motion or petition by one of the parties thereto, made under and in accordance with the act or acts of Congress of the United States, and such motion and petition not being made, all such cases shall be proceeded with in the proper State Courts.

Section 8. Seals of Courts

Upon a change from Territorial to State Government, the seal in use by the Supreme Court of the Territory of Utah, until otherwise provided by law, shall pass to and become the Seal of the Supreme Court of the State, and the several District Courts of the State may adopt seals for their respective courts, until otherwise provided by law.

Section 9. Transfer of Probate Causes to District Courts

When the State is admitted into the Union, and the District Courts in the respective districts are organized, the books, records, papers and proceedings of the probate court in each county, and all causes and matters of administration pending therein, upon the expiration of the term of office of the Probate Judge, on the second Monday in January, 1896, shall pass into the jurisdiction and possession of the District Court, which shall proceed to final judgment or decree, order or other determination in the several matters and causes, as the Territorial Probate Court might have done, if this Constitution had not been adopted. And until the expiration of the term of office of the Probate Judges, such Probate Judges shall perform the duties now imposed upon them by the laws of the Territory. The District Courts shall have appellate and revisory jurisdiction over the decisions of the Probate Courts as now provided by law, until such latter courts expire by limitation.

Section 10. Officers to Hold Office Until Superseded

All officers, civil and military, now holding their offices and appointments in this Territory by authority of law, shall continue to hold and exercise their respective offices and appointments, until superseded under this Constitution: Provided, That the provisions of this section shall be subject to the provisions of the Act of Congress, providing for the admission of the State of Utah, approved by the President of the United States on July 16th, 1894.

Section 11. Election for Adoption or Rejection of Constitution and for State Officers/Voters

The election for the adoption or rejection of this Constitution, and for State Officers herein provided for, shall be held on the Tuesday next after the first Monday in November, 1895, and shall be conducted according to the laws of the Territory, and the provisions of the Enabling Act; the votes cast at said election shall be canvassed, and returns made, in the same manner as was provided for in the election for delegates to the Constitutional Convention.

Provided, That all male citizens of the United States, over the age of twenty-one years, who have resided in this Territory for one year next prior to such election, are hereby authorized to vote for or against the adoption of this Constitution, and for the State Officers herein provided for. The returns of said election shall be made to the Utah Commission, who shall cause the same to be canvassed, and shall certify the result of the vote for or against the Constitution, to the President of the United States, in the manner required by the Enabling Act; and said Commission shall issue certificates of election to the persons elected to said offices severally, and shall make and file with the Secretary of the Territory, an abstract, certified to by them, of the number of votes cast for each person for each of said offices, and of the total number of votes cast in each county.

Section 12. Officers to be Elected

The State Officers to be voted for at the time of the adoption of this Constitution, shall be a Governor, Secretary of State, State Auditor, State Treasurer, Attorney General, Superintendent of Public Instruction, Members of the Senate and House of Representatives, three Supreme Judges, nine District Judges, and a Representative to Congress.

Section 13. Contest for District Judgeship, How Determined

In case of a contest of election between candidates, at the first general election under this Constitution, for Judges of the District Courts, the evidence shall be taken in the manner prescribed by the Territorial laws, and the testimony so taken shall be certified to the Secretary of State, and said officer, together with the Governor and the Treasurer of the State, shall review the evidence, and determine who is entitled to the certificate of election.

Section 14. Constitution to be Submitted to Voters/Ballot

This Constitution shall be submitted for adoption or rejection, to a vote of the qualified electors of the proposed State, at the general election to be held on the Tuesday next after the first Monday in November, A. D. 1895. At the said election the ballot shall be in the following form:

For the Constitution. Yes. No.

As a heading to each of said ballots there shall be printed on each ballot the following Instructions to Voters:
All persons desiring to vote for the Constitution must erase the word "No."

All persons desiring to vote against the Constitution must erase the word "Yes."

Section 15. Election of Officers not Provided for Herein

The Legislature, at its first session, shall provide for the election of all officers, whose election is not provided for elsewhere in this Constitution, and fix the time for the commencement and duration of their terms.

Section 16. When Constitution in Force

The provisions of this Constitution shall be in force from the day on which the President of the United States shall issue his proclamation, declaring the State of Utah admitted into the Union; and the terms of all officers elected at the first election under the provisions of this Constitution, shall commence on the first Monday, next succeeding the issue of said proclamation. Their terms of office shall expire when their successors are elected and qualified under this Constitution.

Done in Convention at Salt Lake City, in the Territory of Utah, this eighth day of May, in the year of our Lord one thousand eight hundred and ninety-five, and of the Independence of the United States the one hundred and nineteenth.

LIST OF DELEGATES:

Done in Convention at Salt Lake City, in the Territory of Utah, this eighth day of May, in the year of our Lord one thousand eight hundred and ninety-five, and of the Independence of the United States the one hundred and nineteenth.

Attest:

JOHN HENRY SMITH, President.

PARLEY P. CHRISTENSEN, Secretary.

Louis Bernhardt Adams
Rufus Albern Allen
Andrew Smith Anderson
John Richard Barnes
John Rutledge Bowdle
John Sell Boyer
Theodore Brandley
Herbert Guion Button
William Buys
Chester Call
George Mousley Cannon
John Foy Chidester
Parley Christiansen
Thomas H. Clark, Jr
Louis Laville Coray
Elmer Ellsworth Corfman
Charles Crane
William Creer
George Cunningham
Arthur John Cushing
William Driver
Dennis Clay Eichnor
Alma Eldredge
George Rhodes Emery
Andreas Engberg

David Evans
Abel John Evans
Lorin Farr
Samuel Francis
William Henry Gibbs
Charles Carroll Goodwin
James Frederic Green
Francis Asbury Hammond
Charles Henry Hart
Harry Haynes
Samuel Hood Hill
John Daniel Holladay
William Howard
Henry Hughes
Joseph Alonzo Hyde
Anthony Woodward Ivins
Wm. F. James
Lycurgus Johnson
Joseph Loftus Joley
Frederick John Keisel
David Keith
Thomas Kearns
William Jasper Kerr
Andrew Kimball
James Nathaniel Kimball
Richard G. Lambert
Lauritz Larsen
Christen Peter Larsen
Hyrum Lemmon
Theodore Belden Lewis
William Lowe Peter Lowe
James Paton Low
Anthony Canute Lund
Karl G. Maeser
Richard Mackintosh
Thomas Maloney
William H. Maughan
Robert McFarland

George Parcust Miller
Elias Morris
Jacob Moritz
John Riggs Murdock
Joseph Royal Murdock
James David Murdock
Aquila Nebeker
Jeremiah Day Page
Edward Partridge
John David Peters
Mons Peterson
James Christian Peterson
Frank Pierce
Wm. B. Preston
Alonzo Hazelton Raleigh
Franklyn Snyder Richards
Joel Ricks
Brigham Henry Roberts
Jasper Robertson
Joseph Eldredge Robinson
Willis Eugene Robison
George Ryan
John Henry Smith
George B. Squires
Harrison Tuttle Shurtliff
Edward Hunter Snow
David Brainerd Stover
Hiram Hupp Spencer
Charles Nettleton Strevell
Charles William Symons
Moses Thatcher
Daniel Thompson
Ingwald Conrad Thoresen
Joseph Ephraim Thorne
Samuel R. Thurman
William Grant Van Horne
Charles Stetson Varian
Heber M. Wells

Noble Warrum, Jr.
Orson Ferguson Whitney
Joseph John Williams

By order of the Convention, May 8th, 1895. JOHN HENRY SMITH,
President